MARKET RESEARCH: A Key Competitive Advantage

Dave Kohl

CONTENTS

INTRODUCTION

Market Research should be a part of any business, whether an individual doing freelance or performance work, part of a multi-million dollar international corporation, or in between. It should never stop.

You need to be finding out all you can about your competition, direct and indirect, and develop the ways to get and stay ahead of them!

It is so very much to your advantage, both personally and professionally, to do this research on your own (within your own business or company) rather than hire an outside firm or contract an individual not already a part of your specific business. You know the business better than an outsider. Your information needs to be kept confidential.

Research is a mind set, not an expense, and is often right in front of us. Let's take the (football) wide receiver who noticed in the first quarter of a game on consecutive plays that he could fake a move to his right and his defender would move in that direction.

He quietly let his coach know how and where he could beat that defender. Did the coach call the next play to make that happen? Of course not. The coach waited until the last few minutes of the game when the game was tied. That is when he called a play in which that receiver faked the defender and got open to receive what turned out to be the game winning touchdown pass!

You could say that the receiver did his research on the defender early in the game by finding out how he could be open. His coach, armed with this important information, knew exactly when to use it. Think about this. If the coach did not have the knowledge about his receiver, he might not have been able to call the play which won the game.

Keep in mind that "Market Research" is not something you need to schedule or assign to a couple hours per week as if it is separate from your daily routine. Think of it as something you should constantly be doing as PART of your daily routine. That includes developing, selling, communicating, bookkeeping, and everything else important to your business or the company you represent.

I do mean constantly, even when it has nothing to do with your business or employment. Your hobbies and personal interests can help you to succeed once you understand what "research" to look for, and add to your fun.

Over the years I have enjoyed reading about some of my favorite musicians in order to find out what makes them tick. Doing so, in addition to hours of musical enjoyment, has actually inspired me on a business level.

Years ago I was reading an interview of one of my favorite performers, in which he talked about his early musical influences. What made this story even more fascinating was when he went on to say that he then went and "researched" these artists. Why? Because he "needed to know" who influenced *them*.

It turns out that he found several of his biggest influences were actually influenced by the same person. Once he found that out, he explored that original influence, and gained significantly from that by researching the "original" source.

While reading a different story about one of my favorite musical groups, I learned that they would send members of their stage crew out into the audience during their concerts acting as typical concert goers. They would scatter and change locations during the shows. Their mission was really to watch and listen to those around them to get their reactions to the various songs. They could see people sitting down, standing up, commenting about the good and the bad, or going to the food stand at certain times, and also monitor the quality of sound and the production of the show itself. That band was able to incorporate positive changes in time for their next shows because of getting this direct feedback they could not otherwise obtain.

Thus, the "Market Research" you need to do for your business is not confined to working hours or to your desk or office. What you are really doing is gathering information, with the next steps being processing and storing that information, and then using as much as you can of it toward growing the business you are in.

1 IDENTIFY YOUR COMPETITION

Every business or individual business person has competition. Even if you are the only person out of 50,000,000 people doing what you do, it would because others have provided something similar for their audience which set the stage for what you are offering.

Suppose you own the only restaurant in town which serves a particular style of food. It does not automatically imply that everyone who likes that style of food will visit twice per week. You are competing with other restaurants for business. The others may not have the food style yours does, but they may have lower pricing, better parking, an easier to reach location, and/or a bigger staff to serve their guests.

A shoe repair specialist (typically) does not sell shoes on a retail basis, and might be only such shop in town. However, if a local retailer chooses to price some of its new shoes low enough to be comparable to repair costs, the repair specialist would stand to lose a portion of his business, which could soon prove fatal.

This is why you need to identify any and all forms of what I term "direct" and "indirect" competition.

Chances are these other businesses consider your business as competition. Let's go back to this most recent example as if you own that shoe repair shop. Suppose a nearby shoe retailer runs a special on new shoes for $29.95 a pair, while your usual cost to repair this style runs about $25.00. It stands to reason that a consumer would prefer to spend "$5 more" for a brand new pair than to repair something they have used many times.

Be aware that the other store developed that sale price as a way to keep local consumers from going to YOUR business. This competing retailer does not offer any repairs whatsoever, and your shop does not sell shoes retail like they do. However, they are holding that sale for the purpose of taking away your "audience" of customers. That makes them true competition.

Of course, if your business is one of three retail shoe stores within a five mile radius, you have a clear cut idea of who your competition is. And starting now, you need to consider shoe repair shops as competitors as well!

This is what I mean by "Identify Your Competition".

Your first step is to make a list of your direct competitors. This depends on whether you do business on a local, regional, national, or international basis. If your products/services are available online, it means that your competition could be anywhere in your country or around the world. It could be a very long and tedious list, but if it is you need to realize what you are up against.

Suppose you have 200 direct competitors. This means that there is and most likely will continue to be a heavy demand for the products/services you are offering. It also means that your initial and then ongoing research could very well produce a ton of ideas which can benefit you directly. And, it means you will get a very clear picture of where your business ranks among them, and how well or poorly you are competing.

Next, make a list, as best you can, of your indirect competition. (Go back to the shoe repair example.) Think of businesses which are targeting the same audience as you are, and compile these as a separate list. The longer your list, the more useful information you will gather.

Your research lists should be thorough. You may or may not investigate every entity you come up with over a period of time. The idea is to be able to best determine which of your direct and indirect competition to be monitoring on a regular basis.

If your business is local or regional (territory, state license, unique attraction, assigned dealer, etc.), look for similar businesses which serve other areas. For example, if you own an ice cream parlor in a cold weather city, finding other similar sized parlors in colder, same weather, and warmer cities, is to your advantage.

Suppose you discover a parlor which is hours away that increased their business last month due to a special coupon your parlor could easily distribute. Your customers would not know of, nor would they travel for hours to participate in, that other parlor's offer. Yet, you could increase your business by implementing this idea, gained because of the secret research you did.

Indirect competition also includes businesses which cater to the same audience yours does but with other products/services. An auto repair business should be tracking auto parts stores (which do not perform repairs) which sell parts for the cars your business can repair, as well as auto paint shops, and any related after market resellers.

The idea is to find, examine, and compare the methods used by your indirect competitors to reach their target audience and grow their business. Next is the ability to incorporate the best methods into your business operation.

2 BEST RESOURCES

Obviously, the internet is likely the most significant resource for finding, identifying, and researching all of these other businesses.

There is more to it than merely coming up with a list of company web sites to explore, although that list is an important first step.

Chances are you already have a list of the primary web site(s) for your direct competitors so that you will be able to enter them into your research database. For example, if your company is ABC Widgets, your list should include DEF Widgets, XYZ Widgets, and so forth.

Next, you need to find the "resource sites" which relate to your business and/or to the competition's. This refers to sites which your target audience is likely to visit, whether they are competitors or related information or entertainment sources.

Suppose your business is or includes online retail sales of automobile parts. You should also be searching for local or regional automobile organizations (such as "Springfield Sports Car Enthusiasts"), upcoming classic car shows and competitions, auto race tracks, and any locally known professional drivers.

By finding and exploring these sites, you will be able to determine your best sites for cross-promotion, advertising, referrals, and/or ideas worth grabbing for your business.

The search engines play a big role in this. Keep in mind that it is always helpful to use more than one search engine, because the result rankings are often different from one to another even with an exact search. You should go with multiple search entries as well, although your first search should be acting as if you are looking to purchase your products or services.

If you operate a men's clothing store in Toronto, your first search could be "men jeans Toronto". Another search, whether you use the same or different search engines, might be "Toronto fashion", "clothing store Toronto", and so on.

Social media should be included. You often do not need to officially "follow" a company in order to see their feeds and comments, but you should do whatever you have to do in order to monitor their activity.

There are plenty more sources in addition to the internet. Local media, such as TV, radio, and newspapers should be checked. Watch, listen, and read stations and sections which appeal to your target audience. It's not about what you personally enjoy. It is where your current and potential customers can be found.

Consider local or national trade associations and related professional organizations. Perhaps there are appropriate trade shows, whether your business participates (booth or table) or not. If your business does not participate, you should attend and visit with all of your direct and indirect competitors. Find out what information they are providing to attendees, as well as what they might be giving away. Note what they are doing to capture names, e-mail addresses, and any other pertinent information. Note any contests or upcoming events they may be promoting.

Be sure to look for promotions and special offers offered, even if the business has nothing to do with what yours does. Think about how your business could benefit. Suppose you own a bakery, and you see a liquor store with a "Wine of the Month" promotion. Your bakery could easily offer a "Pie of the Month" to your regular customers.

Additional methods of researching your competition could include asking employees, friends, and family members to save any mailings they receive for you. Same with seminars or workshops they offer. Even if you cannot attend, there is something to be learned from how and where they market them, how many people (or companies) participate, and how the hosting business benefits.

If you are not already, do your best to monitor your competition's advertising. Do you see TV commercials for them? Hear radio commercials? See their ads in a local newspaper or magazine? See banner ads online? Do they distribute coupons?

3 COMPILING YOUR DATA

In order to compile your lists, perform your research, evaluate your business or company, plan your methods of response, and determine your ongoing research formula, you need a method to track all of the information as well as to maintain your notes and results.

While you can use whatever method you are most comfortable with and still be successful in utilizing the formulas about to be presented, I am going to suggest the least challenging and least costly methods which I have used over the years.

You do not need to purchase or install any computer software or programs whatsoever. Every business is different in some way, and there is no reason to have to adjust your findings to fit someone else's software. You simply need to determine what to "keep" and where to keep it. Knowing and implementing these will make all of your research a faster and easier process before you get started.

"What" to keep is everything you can about your business and how it operates. I learned this from a client who really was a mentor to me back in the late 1980's, before the internet. He owned and operated several businesses over the years, including the two I was hired for.

Having so many different matters to keep track of simultaneously, he literally kept a diary on his desk and had several file cabinets in his office. He would show me how he would write down a recap of every business phone call and written correspondence he made and received each day, and where he would file documents related to each venture in specific file folders within his office.

If he was in contact with XYZ Corporation regarding ordering 1,000 widgets, he could tell you, from looking at his "diary" who he talked with, what about, and what he was told. If they sent him a proposal letter via fax or overnight mail, he could show me a copy of it by pulling it from his files. Observing and learning how and why he did this for years proved far more valuable than the income I generated from the services I provided.

To this day, I use his methods every single day in my work. My sales and marketing duties include my making an average of 250 outgoing phone calls and custom e-mails per working week covering a wide area and going back more than ten years. Yet, when I am at my desk, I can account for every one of those calls, highlighting the most recent one, within 30 seconds.

Knowing how to accomplish this, and the importance of retaining and updating this database, has directly increased my income. It has also made doing my own research much easier.

First, you need to establish your own system for keeping all of your business "information" and your "results". You can do this whether your business has you on the phone, online, behind a counter, in a vehicle, or anywhere else your job or organization requires.

Keeping track of all you possibly can at your business has everything to do with your market research. The more you can track and compare about your business internally, the more you have to compare against what your competitors are or are not doing in the same way. No matter what industry or service you are involved in.

My primary source, specific to my sales efforts, is nothing more than an Excel spreadsheet (or an equivalent). For my sales efforts, I have created several fields for both current and potential clients I contact primarily via e-mail and/or phone.

Spreadsheet fields I use include columns for: company name, person's name, phone number, e-mail address, city or physical location, most recent result, past results, and next scheduled contact attempt. That "result" can be anything such as leaving a voice mail, sending an e-mail, scheduling a phone or in person appointment, being rejected, having more information or a contract requested, or needing to contact another person within that organization.

After each call (or e-mail), I type the result into the field for the business I contacted, including the result and any other pertinent information.

The second part of my system is specific to retaining information about my direct and indirect competition, along with anything else which is related to the operation and success of the business.

For this, I have found that creating and updating an online "notepad" to be the best method, although using a separate Excel spreadsheet also works. The specifics will vary depending upon the nature of your business.

Information to seek and retain most likely would include inventory, services offered, pricing, physical location(s), web site(s), methods of advertising, giveaways and specials, and operation comparisons.

COMPANY	WEB SITE	ITEMS	PRICES
ABC Widget	www ABCWidget	blue, red, orange widgets	$7.99 to $19.99
DEF Widgets	www DEFWidgets	red, orange, green, purple widgets	$6.99 to $22.99
GHI Widget	www GHI Widget	purple, red widgets	$8.99 to $12.99
JKL Widgets	www JKL Widget	brown, blue, red, orange, green, purple	$5.99 to $13.99
MNO Widget	www BuyFromMNO	red, orange, green, purple widgets	$7.99 to $19.99

All of the research data you acquire should be web based and/or on a computer network. Or, at the very least, there should be a scheduled backup to be sure you do not risk losing years of information. In addition, it is advantageous to be able to log in from more than one office, from home, while traveling, and any time you find useful research information.

Once you determine exactly what information you plan to gather and keep, it is best to determine how and where you will maintain and update it moving forward.

Ideally, you will be able to compile research on every aspect of the sales/service process for your company, whether people, online access, or both are involved. For this purpose, tracking those potential customers who do not make a purchase is just as, if not more, important than keeping track of those who do. Eventually, your research should allow you to compare against how your competitors gain and lose out on more business so that you can take advantage of their mistakes!

4 KNOW YOUR OWN COMPANY

Before you explore and identify your competition, you first need to know and track what your business does, which includes operations as well as sales. This goes into your newly formed database to enable you to compare every relevant category against theirs, while none of them has access to this valuable information.

Your database should also include categories it does not currently use, but which competitors do.

For example, if your business does not produce seminars or workshops, but at least one of your competitors does, this becomes an avenue to explore and compare.

Whether or not you need to utilize a database for your products and/or services offered depends upon the nature of your business. There is too big of a range of possibilities to go into details here, whether your business serves consumers, other businesses, or a combination.

However, before you track and compare your company against the competition, you should be aware of your products and/or services as they relate to the following.

Advertising/Promotion: If your business advertises, you need to include every method currently used, along with as much information about what was previously done as you have or can gather. For example, if you did a TV campaign two years ago that failed miserably, enter that information into your database.

This category should include traditional media advertising such as TV, radio, newspaper/magazine, billboards, direct mail, online display or banners, and niche methods such as shopping carts, or in-store ads.

Of course, you need to include all of your social media within your database, with specifics, as a separate field from details about their web sites. You should also include seminars, workshops, sales staff presentations, in-store displays and/or demonstrations, on-location giveaways, contests, and the like, whether your business does these or not.

Web site(s): List each site that your business has, along with the primary features and purpose of each. This is also a broad category, but you should track factors such as whether or not the emphasis is on sales, product information, content (i.e. blog, newsletter), personnel, introducing a new product/service, entertaining, linking to other resources, and so on.

Social Media:

While Social Media tracking is the least challenging of all of your research tasks, it can prove to be one of the most important. You can handle this yourself even if you are not the person that controls what is posted and/or monitors responses.

It could be as simple as regularly visiting your company's Facebook, Twitter, Instagram, and/or other social media pages. Set up your tracking for fields such as a general description of "your" posts, comments, and/or photos.

You should track the dates and times of the posts, as well as the general nature. Are they about a sale, special price, or an incentive to purchase? Are they comments about something in the news or within the community?

Another field should include information about comments or responses from readers, where applicable.

For example, your research database might have, "Jan. 16 – photo of new widget in green – 482 likes – 27 comments with 22 positive – four did not like new size".

Of course, depending up the nature of your company, you should have fields for specific products and services, changes or upgrades, special sales and promotions, and so forth.

The next step is to find and make the same notes about what your competitors post and receive via the social media they use.

An example of a desired result by doing this would be to find that "over the past 90 days, ABC Widget updated their coupon information three times per week while XYZ Widget only provided one coupon.

5 MAKING CONTACT

Making it easy for customers/clients to be able to contact and interact with your business is a lot more important than some executives realize. Think about how you feel in your personal life when you are about to make a large purchase from a company but can't get an answer to what you feel is a very important question.

As simple as this may sound, explore every method of contact for potential clients/customers of your company before you begin to track them.

The more your business is available to current and potential customers/clients, the better off you will be in the long run. Before you examine what your competitors do (or don't do) to handle this, you need to closely examine your business first.

WEB SITE(S): While it is likely an online visitor can make an order/purchase and view product/service information while visiting your site, you need to know what happens when that visitor has a specific question. Having an FAQ page does not always help everyone with an inquiry.

Is there a specific e-mail address or form which allows a visitor to ask a specific question? If so, you need to know who and how providing the answer is handled.

Is there at least one phone number listed for those who prefer to talk with someone? If so, can potential customers speak with a live representative? If not, how soon are calls returned?

Go onto your company's web site(s). On the home page, notice how easy (or challenging) it is to find the essential contact information. Where is a phone number? E-mail address or related contact form? Street address and/or "Locations" list, form, or link?

How, where, and when can they reach your company? If they cannot reach a live person or receive an immediate response, are they told how long it might take before they do?

TELEPHONE:

You should still be aware of how easy or challenging it is for current and potential customers to reach your company. Track the method(s) available to call your business and how such calls are handled. Consider categories such as live person or recorded announcement, how many phone numbers (service, sales, administrative, etc.) are available, and how calls are monitored.

How easily can a potential customer reach a live person? Can that person truly answer their question immediately?

COMPLAINTS & FEEDBACK:

A huge part of your efforts will be to develop ways to find out the complaints specific to your competitors and use them to your advantage. However, your business needs to have all of its ducks in a row before you can do that.

What happens when your business misses a deadline? Provides the wrong order? Ships the wrong product? Leaves a customer standing for 10 minutes with no help?

Currently, when something goes wrong, how is it handled within your business? How and where can a current or potential customer complain? How are received complaints acted upon? And, is there a method for follow up?

By first exploring this within your business, you will find ways to gain an edge over your competitors. Dealing with complaints is really a three step process for any business.

First, there needs to be a method in place for receiving a complaint. As basic as it sounds, many businesses intentionally make it very challenging for customers to complain. They make it difficult to find the "right" person and/or to be able to fully express the concern.

The next part is the immediate response upon receiving the complaint. Is there a required or a specific action taken by your business?

For example, if a customer tells a manager that you are "out of purple widgets", how does he/she respond? The immediate response might be anything from "Sorry, I'm not sure when we will get more. Would a blue one be OK?" to "How soon do you need it? Can I try another store?" and various points in between.

The third part is what I call the "true" result, especially what happens to that specific customer. Do they leave the store with an answer as to how and when they will get that purple widget? And, what happens if one hour later another customer also needs a purple widget? How is that handled?

Although having a plan for handling complaints is not a part of market research, having the best methods and solutions possible to deal with them is. The research part comes in to play when you begin to compare against how competitors deal with similar situations.

Some businesses have a "company" page or handle on their social media. In addition, employees or associates may also have their own separate pages. For example, a TV station would have its own social media pages and following, while several of its on air personalities also have their "own" pages and followers. Unfortunately (from a business standpoint), multiple outlets from the same business are not always coordinated and may require heavier tracking.

Do your best to find out how your competitors deal with complaints or a customer crisis, and enter them into your database. You want to find out those factors which would entice a client/customer to come over to (or return to) your business.

Chances are that in your personal life you have one or more establishments you refuse to do business with. It might be a restaurant that totally messed up an important dinner date or a clothing store that refused to exchange a torn garment after you purchased it.

Next, using this example, think about your current "go to" restaurant or clothing store which was your immediate replacement. What specific reason(s) did you have for CHOOSING that replacement?

In addition to complaints, monitoring general feedback is also very helpful. Business people have varied opinions about online review sites as well as businesses which publish customer comments. Either way, the idea is to seek out as much commentary about your competition, whether positive or negative, and track that information.

A few years back I was involved with a research project which consisted of randomly calling a few hundred residents of a specific community to ask residents some questions about a local restaurant which had recently opened.

Those who were willing to talk, whether they had been there or not, were asked questions along the lines of whether or not they knew about it and if they would go or had visited. If they had already visited this new restaurant, the specific questions they were asked included how quickly they were greeted, how the food was cooked and how the service was, and about the cleanliness of the establishment.

This was given to them in the form of a follow up survey, as if to be sure that the customer had an all around good experience. If the respondent indicated any part of their visit was not a good experience, they were given the opportunity to explain why. Each person, whether they spoke positively or not, was thanked for having visited.

However, there was one important point these local residents were never told. That recently opened restaurant was actually not involved whatsoever in this survey. It was an established competitor which hired that local market research firm to conduct it! That competitor spent several thousand dollars to gain this extremely valuable research.

If you can find one or more solid resources of feedback about your competitors online or by other *existing* sources, you would be, in effect, saving your business thousands of dollars while compiling and tracking similar information.

You can anonymously follow each of your competitors' postings and pages via social media. When you get to researching their key personnel, you can also add their postings and pages to your monitored list.

In addition, outlets such as Facebook and Twitter are often used by clients/customers as sounding boards by frustrated customers, and occasionally for positive feedback and recommendations to friends and family. You may be able to find out how many "likes" a business has, and ideally, who follows them.

For example, if one of your competitors is "XYZ Widget", you should also perform searches on the various social media sites for any and all mentions and comments on "XYZ Widget", above and beyond postings and comments by the company and/or its personnel.

6 TRACKING YOUR COMPETITORS

Now that we have established what you need to have about your business and what to be aware of in researching the competition, the next step is to gather some basic but essential information about it.

Start with the basic facts, such as their location(s), number of years in business, number of employees (or contractors, if applicable), and financial standing. You may wish to carry these facts a step further and keep a ranking in each category if you have multiple direct competitors.

This information will play a role in your future marketing strategy, regardless of whether your business ranks at the top or bottom in a number of categories.

Next, consider the number of products/services/locations each competitor has, and whether they are the same as what your business provides, more, or less.

For example, suppose your business sells red, white, and blue widgets, while a direct competitor only sells red and white widgets but has more locations and more total revenue. Here are two ways to go with this. Your subsequent research should be geared toward finding out how and why 'they' sell more of the red and white widgets than you do. Your subsequent marketing should be pointing out that your company is the "leader" of red, white, AND blue widget sales.

After you enter the data about your company into your research database, you should then do the same for each of your direct competitors.

Take each appropriate business, and enter in their years in business, financial standing (if available or appropriate), specific items and/or services they provide (whether they all relate to your business or not), physical location(s), and web site(s).

It also helps to have what I call at least one "Comparison" field. The specifics depend upon the nature of your business and your competitors, and what is important to yours. This could be whether or not a competitor is larger or smaller, serves a similar or wider geographic area, has more or fewer employees, web sites, or physical locations, and a larger or lesser inventory.

Once you identify the most important competitive factor(s), those should be the field name(s) for your database. You may wish to be able to update it in weeks to come since this could be a means to detect a business plan you can compete with.

For example, suppose you run a single location restaurant and that your "Comparison" database is the menu of five other nearby restaurants. On the first of every month, you look at (and perhaps print out) the menu of each one. By entering and keeping data within your Comparison notes, you will likely notice some important trends. Perhaps, over the course of a few months, you will see that "Restaurant B" raises prices or adds new items every 3 months.

If and as you see such trends over the course of months or years of doing this research, you will be in position to attack your competitors. If you have, for example, reason to believe that "Restaurant B" is going to raise the price of potatoes on June 1st, you could be ready with a "special" on your potato dishes for the first week of June.

WHAT TO TRACK:

You should set up to compare the products and/or services your business offers and the methods or offering them to your target audience with those of your direct competitors.

This includes whether or not customers can purchase one item or multiple items, methods of ordering (physical locations, online, dealers, resellers, phone, fax, etc.). Your information should include methods of payment, including which credit cards, and other factors such as shipping costs and time period of fulfillment if applicable.

Once you have done this, what you do next is to put yourself in the role of being a potential client/customer for the primary product/service your business offers. For example, if your business is a furniture retailer in New York, act as if you are looking to purchase a new recliner chair for your home. Go online and use a search engine. Compare models and prices among three different furniture retailers (in addition to yours).

Take notes about which retailer has the most to choose from, provides the most detailed product descriptions, has the most inventory, the color you most prefer, the closest location, the fastest delivery (and what, if any, the shipping/delivery cost might be).

Once you complete your notes, there are two separate steps which should follow. The first step is to do an honest and realistic approach to what you would do if you really were a potential customer. Which company would you really buy from – and why? Then list specific reasons why you would not choose the other companies. Be sure to include your company in whichever category so that you can compare.

The more reasons you give for your answer, whether positive or negative, the more thorough your future research will be.

Your second step with this information is to examine your company against the competition in each of the major categories. Suppose you are comparing against four competitors. Based on your findings, honestly rank the "best" company in each appropriate category.

Keep in mind that no one else sees your research data. If you think that XYZ Widget has a better selection of inventory and faster delivery than your business, you need to be aware of this so that you can monitor what they do and how they do it.

You need to know what your company is "better" at for your upcoming advertising and marketing. And you need to know what your competitors are "better" at so that you can use your current and future research toward overtaking them.

COMPANY	WEB SITE	ITEMS
BCD Widget Holders	www. BCDHolders	holder all color widgets
EFG Widget Holders	www EFG4Widgets	holders orange widgets
RST Widget Keys	www RSTKeys	holders red, orange, purple widgets
VXY Widget Holder	www VXYNow	custom holders for all colors
OPQ Widget Key	www OPQHolder	holders all color widgets

Here is an example. Suppose your company has the fastest delivery time for your blue widgets, but three of your competitors offer a lower price. For the near future, your company should not be advertising or promoting its prices. It should be promoting "fastest delivery" to its current and potential customers.

With this in place, the immediate focus of your research should be determining and comparing how and why multiple competitors can offer lower prices.

7 ATTACKING THE COMPETITION

There are plenty of external factors which go toward beating your competitors. You need to find as many weaknesses as possible about them. There are ways to do so in addition to those previously mentioned.

In addition for using social media and complaint web sites to look for complaints about your competitors, you should also check Better Business Bureau and local Chamber of Commerce resources.

Other sources may include appropriate trade associations and local business or networking groups.

You should also research your competitors to determine whether or not they are part of a larger business and/or an affiliated product or service.

As mentioned earlier, research similar companies in different territories in search of good ideas you can "borrow". This is a huge part of effective market research.

Your goal is to find at least one niche which will appeal to some or all of your potential customers, whether you utilize what I call "attack advertising" or not. This refers to situations where you use a circumstance to compare your company to the competition, without mentioning them.

Here is an example. A small mortgage lender looking to compete against several much larger and local banks for loans used this for an advertising campaign. "Don't pay commissions. I own the company and am ready to serve you." The ad was followed by the name of his company and his contact information.

His intent was to make consumers think they would pay more at the local bank because bank representatives receive a commission. This concept appeals to many consumers about to make a large financial commitment. The fact is that his company and the banks each generate nearly the same income from a loan regardless of what the bank pays its personnel.

What this lender did was to provide a solid reason for consumers to choose his company over his most direct competition. The "not paying a commission" was his angle. He knew this was a concern of home buyers looking for the best loan deal. You are doing all of this research and tracking in order to find your "angle" for increasing your business and growing your market share.

Suppose you have a retail store in an outdoor shopping mall, but your prices are usually slightly higher than other stores in the area offering the same merchandise. Your research in trying to buy from them reveals that their customers have to pay to park or walk a longer distance to get there. Your advertising and marketing could be based on "Free Parking" or "In and Out Within 5 minutes".

Perhaps you find that the others have Customer Service

available until 8 PM on weeknights. Your advertising approach could be that "We are here until 10 PM for you".

8 GROWING YOUR BUSINESS

As important as advertising and marketing are to your company, good market research can also contribute significantly to its growth. Here are some examples and techniques, whether your business is retail, service, or manufacturing/wholesaling.

Of course, the specific techniques to use vary according to the style of business, your target audience, and your method(s) of generating your revenue.

RETAIL & WALK-IN CUSTOMERS

It doesn't matter if you have sales people on the floor or if it is self-serve and you only have people at the cash register. Even if you have a computer driven inventory database, the fact that "13 large widgets in aisle 3 sold during the week of the 1st through the 7th" is really only one small portion of the research you need in order to improve your business.

You should, from now on, use inventory updates for a lot more than monitoring sales of specific items. If you have a proprietary inventory tracking system, you should add additional "research fields" to your database.

If you have an inventory tracking system which is operated by an outside company (which therefore would have access to your business information), you need to implement your own "additional" database with additional fields created. (This way, no one outside of your company finds any of your private research.)

Our best example is a grocery store. The inventory system you currently have in place will tell you how many of each brand of milk and bread your store(s) sell on a daily or weekly basis.

The idea, using this example, is to take the research to the next level. Suppose one store sold 204 gallons of milk (all brands) on Wednesday. Of those 204 customers only, what was the next most commonly purchased product? (Not brand, but product.) What product finished third?

When you determine the next two most popular products of milk buyers, your next step is to check the physical in-store location of each of those products. Are they each in the same aisle as the milk? Are they near the checkout stand?

Making this determination with your store's most popular items should give you a solid indication as to where your "milk shoppers" tend to go as a priority when they are in your store(s).

Suppose you find that four of the next five biggest sellers are all in Aisle 3. This would raise the question of whether or not it is wise to move a couple of the big sellers to another aisle so that customers would see even more of the items available. Your first step would be to move (for example) the Orange Widgets to aisle 5 for one week and more closely track the sales results.

Your next step is to have someone (employee, friend, yourself) visit the nearest competing grocery stores, and provide you with notes as to the specific aisle locations of those same items in the other stores.

Knowing that your store sold 12% more Orange Widgets when located in the same aisle as the bread than it did the week before is very helpful information. But knowing how and where your competitors have placed these same items is also very important.

As you are doing this, you should be tracking all of this information. The inventory reports, the specific location of the items before and after you moved them, the difference in sales after you moved them, the location of the items at your competitors' locations, and sales reports for the brown widgets you moved to replace the orange ones.

And there is more. This does not yet include your best source of research, which is your customer base. The majority of shoppers don't know where every item they are looking for is located. (Especially if you moved some of them based on the above!) People are often asking store employees for help in locating a specific item. These requests should be tracked as well, and done without the customers being made aware.

Create and place a tally sheet in the back room and/or a location where your employees have access (but customers do not). Include fields such as "aisle number" "male/female" and "item". Ask employees to do their best to report customer requests upon their return to the tally sheet, which the manager changes every few hours. Establish an easy method for collecting these tally sheets on a regular basis from each location, such as scan and e-mail.

Enter the information into your database, preferably in which you can enter by fields which you can also sort. You will then be able to compare customer concerns for each location and monitor trends. Are people asking for nearby items? Are they constantly seeking an item which is two aisles over? Are they asking because the store moved the item(s) in question?

Visit other grocery stores as if you are a shopper. If your stores show a trend that customers cannot find the jelly, look for the jelly in the competitors' stores and see how they make it available compared to your store(s). Enter this information into your database. As the months and years go by, you may also notice seasonal or other trends, providing you with even more information that no one else has.

PROFESSIONAL SERVICES:

Suppose your business is one or more professional services, such as a group of attorneys, accountants, medical, or financial services.

Whether or not your business advertises or not, it is important to monitor and track the process of developing new clients along with maintaining existing ones.

Often times, in this instance, new and repeat business is generated by a need on the part of the potential client/customer at random times (as opposed to consumers needing to shop for groceries on a regular basis).

You need to track all inquiries and contacts and use your database to distinguish between existing and potential new clients/customers via each available method of contact.

For example, each receptionist/secretary/assistant fielding inbound telephone calls for inquiries, appointment scheduling, or information about a product or service, should be using a form of a checklist about each call. This could be something as simple as a printed paper list with a box to check regarding the nature and general result of each call throughout the business day.

You, in compiling this, should be able to tell that "On the fifth of this month, the front desk received 22 phone calls, of which 14 were referred by Joe Widget's office, 4 were referred by Debbie Widget's office, and the other 4 were outside sales or solicitation phone calls".

Ideally, related data will also eventually tell you how many of those 14 "Joe Widget" calls resulted in an appointment, and then how many of those appointments resulted in sales and/or a new client/customer. And, hopefully, which specific methods were used to convert them.

In some instances, your web site(s) may also factor in to this, whether as a result of advertising, referrals, search engines, social media, e-mail inquiries, or a combination of these. Each source of inquiries should be tracked in the same way as phone calls.

If your business is referral driven, your phone representatives and web site (if applicable) should allow for a potential client to tell, enter, or check mark to say the name of the individual or company which referred him/her/them to your business.

As a marketing idea, if this is appropriate, you could implement something along the lines of "Be sure to tell us if you are a Widget Medical Center client!" You want something which encourages a potential client to inform you of the referral source while hopefully making the potential client think they gain an advantage by doing so.

Although it may not be appropriate for your company to reward or even compensate for referrals, it does not matter with regard to this research. You really want to know your best sources of referrals for a number of reasons. The most important reason is really to determine your best sources for additional referrals.

"John" represents a financial services group which specializes in Retirement Planning. His office has received several nice referrals from "Attorney Joe", whose office handles legal matters specific to estates and family disputes. In return, John refers his clients with legal questions to Attorney Joe as a courtesy.

Put yourself in the role of "John". Your "research" should be geared toward finding other law firms, within your service area, which also handle estate planning and family disputes. Visit their web sites as if you are also interested in Estate Planning.

When a particular law firm offers it, compare their content and methods of attracting clients to what your business does, noting what you think is better along with where you think you have them beat. These firms are indirect competition, since they are seeking a similar audience although not providing the same services.

After you explore their methods, you should contact them about a cross-referral program similar to what you already have with "Attorney Joe" (but without any mention of that). It costs nothing for either company to refer the other.

If and as you develop a cross referral program with more than one such law firm, your web site (or phone presentation, etc.) could easily reference something like, "Can we help with a family dispute?" Perhaps you would eventually have three or four family dispute law firms you could provide for your clients, and let them choose the one they like best. You are doing your client base an additional service when needed, referring business to other firms in return, and you have increased your potential client base at little to no outside marketing cost!

When a law firm you are checking into does not offer Estate Planning, you could still contact that firm. Let that firm know of your expertise in Retirement Planning, and suggest a cross promotion or referral program to them and their specialty.

Don't forget to track your findings either way. Include fields for what you like or don't like about the various law firms' web sites, social media, and methods of contact and response.

MANUFACTURER/WHOLESALE:

A few years ago, I was hired by a manufacturing company to help to expand their client base. Their business was manufacturing specific varieties of springs. At the time, approximately 80% of their business was providing specific springs to auto manufacturers. The other 20% came from other manufacturers in a variety of industries. This company was located within an industrial park area near numerous other manufacturers, warehouses, and wholesalers. When I asked one of the owners how many of "the other 20%" were within five miles, he said, "None. I never thought about that!"

My next step was to develop a sales strategy specifically targeting the largest manufacturers in that community. Because of the proximity, my client was "now" able to offer custom springs to local manufacturers that might have a need, with the very important ability to eliminate shipping time and costs while providing faster service.

Compiling a local database was simple. I knew some of the nearby manufacturing companies from driving around the area. Others were found online. From a list of 22 other manufacturers within a 10 mile radius, an executive of the spring company identified those which do or possibly could incorporate one or more types of custom springs they could produce.

Of course, after the first local client was acquired, my next step was to research the new client's competition. It didn't matter if these others were "local" or not. The marketing angle THEN became that we had "ABC Widget as a client because of our price and service, and we can do the same for XYZ Widget, no matter where it is located".

What about those local manufacturers which did not need our springs? They became a part of my database just the same. Perhaps they will receive an RFP in the future which requires using springs. It is possible they have other industry connections which might have a need. Maybe there is a product or part they are currently producing which could be converted to using custom springs that could save them money and/or production time.

Instead of discarding 20 out of 22 contact attempts as "not going anywhere", the idea is to save the "result" for future consideration.

9 GAINING ADDITIONAL BENEFITS

While growing your company is the most important reason to perform regular research and track the results, there are other competitive advantages to be gained from tracking all you can about the operation of each of your direct competitors.

Although we are suggesting a monthly routine, this could vary based on the nature of the business or service you represent.

You should always be monitoring the web site(s) specific to your competitors. In addition to their sales process, also watch for any updated information and resources, as well as how frequently (or infrequently) they provide new and/or updated information. Then compare with your site(s).

Watch for any new products or services they add, as well as anything they remove from your previous visit.

If they have physical locations (stores, dealers, etc.), be sure to track the number of them so that you can be aware of any new additions and/or closings. Some companies which expand each year will show "new locations" or "coming locations", which is extremely valuable to discover as soon as possible for your planning.

In addition, monitor them for employment opportunities,

and track them. Over a period of time you should be able identify some important points about them. Does XYZ Widget have a big turnover? Do they seek less experience for their personnel than your hiring standards? Perhaps you find out that they have hired four production managers within the past year. You may also be able to compare the hiring processes.

The information you gain from this can help your business in several ways in addition to refining your sales, service, and/or inventory process well beyond your advertising and marketing. The idea is to find at least one "weakness" to exploit to your advantage.

Here are some examples. Suppose you find that XYZ Widgets is looking to hire a Night Manager, although they currently do not have a night shift. This would tell you they are looking to expand. If DEF Widgets has discontinued a product line, there might be someone with expertise in that product now looking for employment that could help your company.

Suppose DEF Widgets have just closed one location (while keeping others). You could then plan an advertising campaign geared toward their former customers in that community to alert them to your nearest location. Or perhaps look into temporarily taking over their location in order to convert those customers into your customers.

If a competitor has discontinued a couple of product lines or services which are not doing well for your company either, this could be a reason for your company to also discontinue, knowing that you will not lose market share to your biggest competitor if you do.

CUSTOMER	MOST RECENT	ITEMS	AMOUNT
Bob Black	7/4/2015	3 brown widgets	$18.45
Gil Green	7/4/2015	6 blue, 6 white, 6 red widgets	$42.25
Rod Red	7/3/2015	10 orange widgets	$63.27
Bonnie Brown	7/3/2015	5 blue, 4 orange, 3 purple widgets	$38.15
Paula Purple	7/3/2015	1 blue, 1 red, 1 purple, 2 green widgets	$22.48

What I call "New Business Development" is important to any business, and the research database you maintain will be a huge part of it. You can discover important information from your efforts, although there are times when simply listening can help. Personally, there have been numerous times when I have sent myself a text message with an idea I saw another business (or business person) doing that I could adapt to mine.

Sometimes, simply monitoring the competition or other businesses you are in contact with can be used to your advantage. We all know that things can go wrong, whether technical or personnel issues or mishaps.

There is the story of "Jason", who found out that his competitor's web site for Joe's Widgets, had crashed that morning. By doing his research, he had contact information for several of Joe's Widgets' customers (who he was trying to get for his business) already in place. He was then able to immediately send them an e-mail, with a link to his order page, to let them know that "You can order your Widgets from us today and until Joe's is able to restore its only order function", and his complete contact information.

Chances are that the Joe's Widget customers receiving the e-mail will visit the Joe's site, and see that it is down. If any of those customers need to order, Jason will get the business. Even if they are not, they now think positively about Jason's company for trying to help them.

Keep in mind that if Jason did not have that database ready to go and had not done his research, this opportunity would have been lost. And, if he was not made aware of the problem with the Joe's Widgets web site, he would have not had the opportunity. Of course, none of us have time to check for this constantly, but it shows the benefits of regularly monitoring the situation.

If and when you learn of a situation such as this, even if you cannot react (like the example), note it in your database. Being the only one keeping such information could help you down the road.

10 CONCLUSION

You should compile your lists, specific to your business, of what to keep track of and which companies to monitor on a regular basis. Remember to include indirect competitors.

It is important to consistently perform your research, and to maintain your private database of information over the following months and years.

The information you gather can help your advertising and marketing, hiring, expansion, and overall growth.

Keep this in mind when determining the priorities for your business, as well as for implementing specific strategies and making budget changes.

In addition, if this applies, keep this in mind for RFP's and Business Development Proposals. The more facts you can put in which put your company in a better light than the competition, the better off your company will be. For months and years to come.

ABOUT THE AUTHOR:

Dave Kohl brings his 30+ years of sales, marketing, and project management experience along with his secrets to success in the business world. One of his first tips in the business world was knowing to "keep track of everything". He literally kept a diary of his phone calls and proposals before there were computers to help him.

Mr. Kohl, chosen as "Business Person of the Year" by the Los Angeles Area Chamber of Commerce (1990), personally sold more than $10,000,000 worth of online, radio, television, newspaper, and magazine advertising during the 10-year period (2005 through 2014) leading into the completion of "Market Research: A Key Competitive Advantage".

He has also created industry specific seminars and workshops, along with seven semesters of teaching broadcasting at Columbia College Chicago during the 1990's. This followed several years of radio broadcasting for stations in Chicago and other markets.

Kohl's previous book, "8 Hours To Sell Your Home", is also available in Audio Book form, taking literally eight hours to listen to. It takes home owners every step of the way from considering selling to strategies for fixing, pricing, hiring the right agent, and riding herd until the sale is complete.

Since 1992, Kohl has served as Marketing Director of Chicago area based First In Promotions Inc., an advertising and marketing firm with an emphasis on real estate marketing.

DAVE KOHL

www.ingramcontent.com/pod-product-compliance
Lightning Source LLC
Chambersburg PA
CBHW071124210326
41519CB00020B/6409